# Poetry Potpourri

## A Colorful Journey

Carolyn J. Mollica

**BALBOA**.PRESS

A DIVISION OF HAY HOUSE

Balboa Press books may be ordered through booksellers or by contacting:

Balboa Press
A Division of Hay House
1663 Liberty Drive
Bloomington, IN 47403
www.balboapress.com
844-682-1282

Because of the dynamic nature of the Internet, any web addresses or links contained in this book may have changed since publication and may no longer be valid. The views expressed in this work are solely those of the author and do not necessarily reflect the views of the publisher, and the publisher hereby disclaims any responsibility for them.

The author of this book does not dispense medical advice or prescribe the use of any technique as a form of treatment for physical, emotional, or medical problems without the advice of a physician, either directly or indirectly. The intent of the author is only to offer information of a general nature to help you in your quest for emotional and spiritual well-being. In the event you use any of the information in this book for yourself, which is your constitutional right, the author and the publisher assume no responsibility for your actions.

Any people depicted in stock imagery provided by Getty Images are models, and such images are being used for illustrative purposes only. Certain stock imagery © Getty Images.

Print information available on the last page.

ISBN: 978-1-9822-5390-5 (sc)
ISBN: 978-1-9822-5391-2 (e)

Balboa Press rev. date:  10/21/2020

# CONTENTS

In the world of literature, poetry has always risen to the apex of quintessential thought. Shakespeare, Donne, Blake, Dickenson and Poe have asked us to delve deeper, to uncover the joy and sorrow which words can express. Although the following poems are a mixture of reverie, joy and a bit of horror, they seem relevant to the schismatic and troubled world we share. Hopefully, my poetry will lift your spirit and comfort your soul!

I only ask one thing of my readers – to look beyond the dirty windows or outer appearances to see the wonderful world before us, the picture beneath, and delve deeper to uncover the hidden truths.

I dedicate this book to my grandfather, Joseph A. Hug, who was blessed with intelligence, persistence, and a positive attitude. My grandfather was an educated accountant but an amputee from diabetes who continued working in New York City after World War II. Yes, Joseph Hug, was like his unique last name, a man who embraced life with incredible optimism. As a doting granddaughter, I repeatedly asked: "Why Papa, do you scratch your wooden leg?" His response was always, "I feel it, even though it is gone." That unexplainable truth fascinated me!

The poems in the following pages are examples of the many inexplicable realities I have encountered as the mother of seven successful children and twelve grandchildren, a retired professor, teacher and tutor!

Franz Kafka said it so well: "Poetry is always an expedition in search of truth." Join me in my journey - looking back but always up!

# THE OPTIMIST

I saw the face of God
I saw it seven times . . .
Each time a babe was lifted -
From my womb to my arms.

It wasn't in the Book.
I did not find it there . . .
The child saw me as God,
And I saw it as rare

The vision didn't last
It clouded with the years . . .
Yet each time, I hold a child,
The Miracle re-appears!

# BEAUTIFUL BUTTERFLY

Beautiful butterfly, you dance in the air
With gossamer wings, you land everywhere
Won't you land on my shoulder or my hand?
Open and close your wings like a fan?
Gather the nectar from each pretty flower
I'll watch you in sunlight or in midst of a shower
Multicolored – orange, blue, green and brown
If only I could catch you on the ground
Beautiful butterfly, spread those patterned wings
I'm positive that when you appear, an angel sings!

# HEAVENLY HUMMINGBIRD

Heavenly hummingbird, you are Nature's prize in every way,
Fluttering from flower to flower . . .
Tell me - How much nectar can you suck in an hour?
Wings like window wipers at high speed,
You are the jewel of my garden, I've come to need
At dawn or dusk, you are a visual treat
Yet catching you on my phone - is quite a feat!
On hollyhocks, succulents and zinnias - you may appear
How I wish or hope, I could be near!
Do you really visit 1,000 flowers each day?
Fly thirty miles an hour as some say?

You are a myriad of colors –
Blue, green, yellow with a long beak
Sucking the nectar is a magical feat
That sugar not only pollinates
But contradicts fatigue with an endless beat
It's magic!! How your wings endlessly flutter and flap
When, if ever - do you take a nap?
I wait at my feeder to meet you, unsure
Your appearance excites me
It is so Divine . . .
Of course, you delight me! I want to see more!

# WICKED AND WILD

Wicked and wild, I wish I were . . .
Only the curses, I would slur,
Conscience crushed, if only I could
Thirty lovers? I certainly would

But woe to the moral maiden here!
A ghastly specter harbors near . . .
To quaff rising heat and flame.
Purple passion and desire – tame!

The Soul censors the body's search . . .
Unabashed abandon and Lust besmirched
Only in dreams can this psyche soar.
Wicked and wild, the senses say -
      "More!"

# SECRETS

Secrets are closets in which we do hide …
All the demons and negatives we have inside
Secrets? We All have them
And keep them so safe!
But - What would happen if they would escape?
To tell the world you are weird or plain "odd."
Your life with Richard is just a façade . . .
Your nose had surgery . . . Your face had a lift,
You never loved your job, and hated that birthday gift!
You bought your acceptance . . . Your degree was a phony
Even your *summa cum laude* was really baloney!
Your Siamese cat can tell us the truth
Better than Holmes, the famous sleuth
Here's to the truth tellers!
Let's give them a toast!
Unsung heroes who never boast . . .
Should I admit I am balding or have no teeth of my own?
No real royal blood to claim the throne
Should I say "Forgive me, I lie all the time?"
Or drown my sins with a bottle of wine?
Perhaps, I can finally free my soul with confession
Because, in reality,
SECRETS are my obsession!

# WHEN I'M PAST NINETY . . .

### (Dedicated to Emily Dickenson)

When I'm past ninety, I know what I will do . . .
I'll smoke marijuana and make great Irish stew.
When I'm past ninety, I know what I will say.
The filthy F'***g curses, I can't say today.

When I'm past ninety, I'll sunbathe in the nude.
Do you think by 2040, they'll really think I'm lewd?
When I'm past ninety, I'll be slim and tall . . .
Crass critics will comment - "She's got no ass at all!"

When I' m past ninety, I'll have sex every day . . .
And if you care to notice, my lover won't be grey.
When I'm past ninety, each minute will be mine . . .
I'll bind my poems with ribbon, not ordinary twine!

# DESIRE

Legs entwine . . .
Lips pursue
Purple passion, I never knew
Flesh tingles to the touch
Breathing quickens
Too, too much!
Strobing lights
Pulsating parts
No reason restrains
Foolish hearts

Two lovers in the shower
Why not- every hour?

# THE SNOB

(Dedicated to Sheldon Silverstein)

It's not my fault, I am a snob
My parents made it so . . .
I never touched the sand on the beach,
Surely, NEVER shoveled snow . . .

I never drank from a paper cup,
I seldom carried weight . . .
I always got a ride to school or work . . .
A bright future was my fate!

My hair was coifed, my clothes were all designed . . .
My reputation was never challenged or maligned . . .
My diction and manners? You guessed - beyond compare

Yet one rainy day . . .
Just across from the Plaza or was it the Pierre?
I slipped on poop and screamed for help . . .
Shouting - "Dammit"
"That's so unfair!"

# FAÇADE

I saw a child sitting there -
A blonde child with hyacinth hair.
A petite miss without a care -
A golden girl with skin so fair.

She saw me too and batted her eyes -
She looked back down and heaved three sighs.
That pretty child with eyes so green -
That sweet child could never be mean!

I saw her smiling with the strangest look -
I caught her grimacing in the brook.
The nimble nymph near the water's edge -
That agile child who danced on the ledge.

She twirled and sang a silly song -
Trilled on her toes a minute long.
That tippy-toed tot could hypnotize me -
The melodious moppet mesmerized me!

She wore a white dress and bonnet too -
Her ribbon sash was bonny blue.
The colorful lass made me so gay -
The wee waif took my cares away!

Suddenly, she opened her mouth so wide -
A fiery-eyed eel spumed from inside.
That precious child who heaved three sighs -
That carefree girl with the innocent eyes.

She vomited and vomited - a slippery sluggish snake!
I watched in horror . . . worried for her sake.
The tormented child made an awesome scene -
The possessed waif who seemed serene.

She turned to me, held out her arms -
With a yearning and burning plea.
To save her from the darkest charms -
Of a damned soul's agony.

I turned and ran with all my fear -
But, not a step could I retreat.
The scene ensnared my mind and soul -
Escape was my defeat!

I could not run . . . I could not hide . . .
What had she done?
The seed's inside!

Now I sing a silly song . . .
And seem serene all day long . . .
Onlookers watch me wistfully too . . .
If only they knew! . . . If only they KNEW!

# THE SEMIOTIC PARADOX

I know a mellifluous mentor
Whose speech is clipped and careful,
Charismatic, yet calculated,
Articulate yet conservative.

But his body language defies this . . .
With smoldering sensuality,
Unabashed abandon
Uninhibited motion.

He straddles his chair,
Smooths his grey hair . . .
And strips with his eyes

Which is real?
Which is a facade?
Does this dichotomy make sense?
It is certainly odd.
Perhaps, he is like Donne,

A priest with great passion
Who woos his audience
In his idiosyncratic fashion?

# MY CULINARY PASSION
# – VEAL SCALLOPINI

You will need Marsala plus a 1 ½ lbs. of veal
Parsley, salt & black pepper will give this dish its zeal
First dredge the cutlets with flour . . .
Sauté in garlic & olive oil with love . . .
Add ½ cup of beef bullion & sprinkle with leaf parsley
To embellish with some green
Cook for ten minutes; now taste with your wooden spoon
Mmm . . . so delicious – With this Sicilian dish, you'll swoon
Sliced baby portabellas? Those you save for last!
A triple splash of Marsala
Now dish, then serve this the sublime entrée
From which no guest could possibly fast!

# THINGS ITALIAN ("COSA ITALIANE")

Everything Italian seems so sublime
From the Vatican & Sistine Chapel to linguine with wine
I love every movie Fellini and De Sica make
Biscotti for breakfast, gelato later, not cake
I love Tuscan vineyards, leather goods, and Etruscan gold
The Amalfi coast and Positano are sights to behold
Tall, dark and handsome, give me a break!
for Goodness sake!
Have you seen Michelangelo's David or Bellini's fountains
Crossed the Ponte Vecchio or climbed the Apennine Mountains?
Italian music and the language – surely give you joy
"Ragazza" or "ragazzo" is just a girl or boy
Watch "Cinema Paradiso"; you will learn the art of kissing
Italians love life. You don't know what you're missing!

# WHAT MAKES A DIFFERENCE TO A CHILD

What a difference it makes, to see what they see . . .
Squat down at their level or bend that knee,
Allow the child to make mistakes -
Spill the batter – mispronounce a word . . .
Color outside the bolded lines
Children say it many times

Did they paste those cutouts upside down?
Let it be . . . Don't criticize or judge with a frown
A daisy is there for picking
To count from 1 to 10 . . .
The mint is there for sniffing
Or sharing with a friend

Take a walk with a toddler,
Discover what they see or hear
Delight may be far away - or oh, so very near!
Listen to what they ask!
What was the best part for them? - not you!
Could be at the library, museum or zoo.

"Why?" - Children ask, day after day!
The answer may be on YouTube today
Encourage kids always to do or dare!
And when there is no answer . . .
You can teach a simple **Prayer!**

# FAMILY FORGIVENESS

Why should we forgive the abuse we have endured?
Who should be punished for the violence and the pain?
Yes, the guilty deserve to suffer . . .
But, your anger and torment are just in vain!

They may continue in their devil deeds . . .
While you suffer the corrosion your hatred feeds . . .
When you finally realize, the idea is to let it go
Free your mind to soar and invest in better things . . .

Surely, the hatred you hold onto, makes you sick and sad . . .
Yet, the one it is directed at is unaware you're mad.
So, burn your thoughts in a bonfire . . .
                              Dispose of all the ash!
Your investment in love will free you,
                         To the higher road, FREE at last!

# ODE TO SENIORS

If you're like me – you avoided getting old . . .
Exercised, worked long and hard, bought anti-aging products sold!
"Retired, not retarded," inappropriately my sister-in-law used to say . . .
"I'm fine," "Can do it myself" "I can find my way!"
But if you are not one of us, you'll Never understand . . .
All the things you did before? Now? Definitely banned!
We drive too slow, . . . eat too much . . . never get it right!
Our minds, once sharp, our words now lost, even our eyesight!
Our backs and knees need extra help; we take a pill for pain
We read and watch TV, but can't remember the actor's name!

Our mothers, fathers, favorite friends have literally passed on!
We want to share fond memories, but those that remember? Gone!
Our wise advice is meant to help, but the younger do not hear . . .
They have to learn for themselves, and deaf to words we fear.
Have we gotten too lazy and lascivious with our abundant wealth?
I believe there is hope . . . It is just around the bend . . .
Give kindness where there is little; kind words can surely mend!

Anne Frank told us to believe in spite of all the doom
She had such hope for all mankind amidst the dark and gloom
There is hope!
Have faith!
Be kind!
Love deeply while you are here!
You have the power of numbers to change the world indeed,
Seniors pray and encourage all others . . .
The hate will disappear!

# THE CATHEDRAL

Isn't it ethereal? The spires touch the sky.
Like the hands of the prayerful, they too question Why?
Is the church merely a building?
A sanctuary from all the world's madness?
Or is the Church, we may question
An institution? With dogma, some corruption and sadness?
Perhaps, it is a body of people who seek that ecstasy
Of being close to Christ and perhaps, worry free

I love the Gothic splendor,
The windows that reflect the light . . .
Those stained-glass segments,
Depicting stories do delight . . .
Of course, we know the beauty is all a facade
That God tells us . . . there is so much more,
A home in heaven awaits the worthy to explore!

# ENOUGH ALREADY

Klickity Klock, Rickity Rock
Oh, by Golly, I lost my sock . . .
Heavens to Betsy! What will I do?
I found my sock, but lost my shoe
I found my shoe, but lost my keys
Mother Mercy – Help me please!

I called my son; he cut me short
I drank a tumbler of Spanish port
I texted my daughter; she answered
"What is this? It makes no sense
       Something is amiss"

I petted my dog. He licked my face
My lipstick got smeared. I looked a disgrace
I guess I'm really having a bad day!
Do you think it's because my hair is grey?
I tried to color it with Clairol's best
Being a senior sucks! You may have guessed!

# THE MOVIE BUFF

Do you watch movies with a tub of popcorn with your spouse?
Or is movie night your escape with the kids on the couch?
Are old Classics your "cup-of-tea" or is HBO your specialty?
Some adults love foreign films for their narative and theme
Kids love animation and Disney characters are their dream
Americans sure love cars and spy series seem to be number one
Seniors all agree - horror and zombies are no fun
Some us us return to the same film so many times
Others are addicted to Neflix series and fascinated by crimes
Whether "Sleepless in Seatle" or "Rear Window" is your pick
"The Exorcist," "Annabelle" and "Hannibal" are truly sick flicks!

Some love "Chicago" or "Hamilton" to dance to Broadway tunes
Others make us queezy, when Henry XIII and Ann Boleyn resumes
There's a movie for every culture, every person young or old
With adjustable sofa lounge seats, tickets are often presold
Some features move us to tears and soften hardened hearts
Others move us to reevaluate our previous political smarts
An art form which is ubiquitous and soothes our worst fears!
"Life is Beautiful" and "Cinema Paradiso" can bring us all to tears . . .
But if you need to laugh, "Uncle Buck" or "Home Alone" will do the trick
After which, "Pulp Fiction" or "Man on Fire" may make you sick!

Spielberg, Eastwood, Tarantino and Kassinski may please you
Clearly great directors, but Katherine Bigelow and Greta Gershig are quite new

When it comes to heart breakers? Of course, there is Brad Pitt
De Niro, Depp, Damon, & Vitomiglia, charming - you must admit
Women include Streep, Sarandon, Jolie, Blunt, Garland & Stone
To remember all the names, you'll need an Apple iPhone
Cinema helps students know the classics without the book
A movie buff like me - just never forget to look!
So join the aficionados who watch at least one film a day
You'll find yourself never at a loss of something witty to say!

# IN DEFENSE OF EMILY DICKINSON

I know I will meet her someday
And I'll wear a white dress too!
We'll talk of our inhibitions . . .
Our taboo points of view

Our carriage will be drawn by mustangs
And we will hold the reins
No restraints or punctuation rules
In hindsight, Higgins and critics will be fools

Some historians will think our coziness is gay
Not recognizing our deeper insight of our earthly stay
We need no organized religion!
We will laugh at all who frown
No politics nor powerful men can ever put us down!

Yes, Emily, you will find me as mundane as you
When we discover the truth for all . . .
Respect Mother Nature; revere each and every man
See no imperfections! But love all if you can!

# ENGLISH IS CRAZY

English is crazy, don't you agree?
With cinnamon and synonym, you see.
There's fiancé and fiancée for the man or the girl
But resume and resumé set me in a whirl!
I thought English had no accents . . .
But the rules make my hair curl!
I know how to pronounce the French derivatives
Like depot, valet, and ennui - to name a few
The elitist French we borrow - make an impossible vocabulary stew

English is crazy; it's so very hard to learn
If I misspell "receive," my teachers act so stern
What is the difference between knight and night?
One rides a horse; the other's a beautiful starry sight!
One who can spell "psychiatrist" must have a special brain
"Sikiatrist" seems just as good and comb should drop that "b"
My teacher claims words with long vowels end in the letter "e"

I would change all spelling; simply spell what you hear!
So - Ruff and tuff would drop the "ough"
The endings could be easy!
I'd spell electrician, action and division one way!
Make "shun" here to stay! Pronunciation is confusing.
We should pronounce like words the same!
Prefixes and suffixes are as screwy as can be
Starts and endings could be as simple as 1, 2, 3
We could say "marry" and "unmarry" instead of the word "divorce"
Mount and unmount - if we ride a horse
No one cares a corkscrew for Champagne except the French
Plus "hors d'oeuvres" with "pâté de fois" can have a slight stench
You see - there is a conundrum because dilemma is too hard to spell

A "problem" or "puzzle" is something we can solve
But "enigma" and "labyrinth" are much too involved
Yes, English gives us 50 words, when all we need in one!
"Obese, rotund, corpulent, stout and pudgy"
Basically mean - that person weighs a ton!
We could simply say "chubby" It would be more fun!

Be pleased if you're called "intelligent" "smart," or "brilliant" too!
Because "sly," "cunning," or "shrewd," may cause one to sue!
Spendthrift and parsimonious confuse me every time . . .
Thrifty or not? Does parsimonious mean divine?


Yes, English is not easy, known well to so very few!
Take a course in grammar and you'll forget all you knew!
Who or Whom? "That or Which?" Do I really need to know?
Only pedantic professors spend hours with their bombastic show

English is crazy! I think you all agree!
A futile endeavor to spell, or speak it PERFECTLY!

# THE VALUE OF AN EDUCATION

School is certainly fantastic, depending on where you stand . . .
For parents, it's a respite or like a movie-on-demand
It allows them to go to work, attend meetings and see a shrink
For students, it's demanding to read, write and think!

It always comes with mandates, like homework or projects due
Students are extra busy, some parents and tutors too!
School has its advantages and a box of handy tools
Without a dictionary, thesaurus and search, most of us are fools

School represents the education all counselors recommend
After 12 years of preparation, college applications we must send
Then we start all over . . . deciding what is our major
Skipping a semester, would do most of us a favor

Should we pursue medicine, law, engineering or design?
Indecision and boring classes may boggle some student's mind
Which field will earn good money? Should they help the world at large?
Should I go "pro bono" or exaggerate what will I charge?

There are many blue and white collared workers
Plumbers, electricians, builders and business owners too
Without the diploma but a steady income and positive point of view
We all can't be scholars; we all can't get that 4.0 GPA
Our firefighters and EMS workers have a very special brotherhood they say
An education may be a ticket to a better life indeed
Just remember - there are many kinds of diplomas
And so many ways to succeed!

# MINUTIA

I am not sure why, but I love all things small
From the baby blooms in vases to tiny photos on my wall
I love the little touches of decorations overlooked
Even mini braids or tassels on a prayer book
I watch the tiniest creature crawling away from me
I love the fluff of a dandelion, pollywog from the tree
The feather left behind, the single white snowflake
When winter has already changed its tune
Or when the sun is merely a sliver on the horizon
And I see the crescent of the moon
My joy is in the character toothpicks, not the sandwich or cookie tray
So why do I have this obsession with things so very small?
Perhaps, I wish to be a part of the microcosm of all things
To cure these viruses a miniscule pathogen brings
"To see the world in a grain of sand"
Those were Blake's words, not mine
But living small, but stoically would be fine
There's a wee crack in the doors to heaven
I am positive I will slip through
Not because I've been a saint
But did small acts of kindness – Only my Creator knew!

# A TRUE FRIEND

A true friend is a blend of kindness and criticism held in check
One wishes to say "Don't do that . . . it will make you sick!"
But, you hold your breath
One friend is on a seesaw, riding the high and low
The other is enjoying the vississitudes no matter where they go!
Sometimes a friend has such faith in your success . . .
You wouldn't have the heart to disappoint or cause him or her distress
Can we as friends let go when there are wrong decisions?
Ignore the piccadillos and move on?
It is the peace of our communion - a very special bond?
We share some inconsequential chatter and some that is supreme
We cherish each others hopes . . .
We wish each others dreams . . .
We sing each others songs and dance without restraint
We bring out the best in each other
Our memories are intertwined
Our lives are forever a patchwork quilt
No outsiders can decipher the love designed!

# 2020 PANDEMIC

Why? We all ask, has this pandemic cursed our earth?
Could it be something we all deserved?
Some believe it is Armageddon with numbers of deaths unheard!
It didn't come so sudden because there were signs . . .
Scientists certainly knew!
SARS, AIDS, Ebola and Zika have killed millions, not just a few
Why is 2020 such a horror to all in quarantine?
Are those defiant to the law justified or are they just very mean?
What is so hard to hear and heed?
Wearing masks should be a simple act
Yet thousands of Americans are denying the simple fact
Supposedly, the defiant believe their freedom has been breached
Deaf to all the warnings of the CDC or speeches Fauci speaks
No care for those around them, or for the danger they bring home
Present at weddings, funerals, birthdays, and even at houses of worship
                    they still roam . . .
What happened to "Family first"? What happened to "love one another"?
Social distancing should be for all - not only for a brother
Our world has become so greedy for material things like phones
We ignored the suffering of the poor and deaf to the homeless moans
Respect our seniors, doctors, nurses, and first responders who really care
Perhaps then, & only then, will this end the Covid-19 Nightmare!

# PRONOUN CONFUSION?

I am totally confused, I am a girl
This pronoun dilemma has me in a whirl
I am wondering how to address this one
Who started as a daughter or son . . .
Whatever sex this person wishes is correct
So, if Eric is now Chantelle, use she or her
If Jennifer is now Bradley, use he or him
But making a mistake is a definite sin!
But what do we call someone who is not sure?
Does he and she go out the door?
"Genderqueer" does not sound nice
But, I actually googled this twice.
Ze/hir/hirs is correct but "they" may make us all upset
Isn't "they" plural and we are talking about a single human?
Perhaps to distinguish I will need to zoom in
Our world is a jumble for many of us, you see
Not only for seniors, but anyone older than three!

# IT'S NOT TOO LATE

It's not too late; the earth's problems have a cure
Pandemic, global warming and racial bias, and some more
Who hasn't polluted our land, our air or our water?
Brought innocent creatures and animals to slaughter?
We have chopped down trees and raped our forests
Mined for natural resources from land and sea
Poisoned our fish with discarded plastic, you must agree
Yes, in merely a century, our world has truly diminished
Our wildlife extinct, the Arctic ice is practically finished
Dividing the world like the imaginary Equator line
Borders, boundaries and walls seem just fine
North from South, East from West, segregation is a quest
Politics? We could go far left or right
Détente & coexistence seem out of sight
We seemed to abandon all hope even God
Our conscience or moral compass– a mere façade
We seemed to let go of our dreams in a flash
Turned our attention to materialism and cash
If we allow hatred and xenophobia to brew within
We are all quite capable of committing great sin
Acts of kindness can lead to salvation
We all know selfishness insures damnation
Cherish your family, your heroes, your time
It is time to lift that blanket of doom
Not next month or next year, but soon, very soon
Give of yourself and all will be fine
Peace will return and worries will wane
All your good deeds will not be in vain!

# GIGGLES

There is nothing like the sound of Giggles
To set you in a spin
That contagious swoosh of laughter
Much, much stronger than a grin
Usually it sets in motion, without much thought or design
Just a silly AHA moment
We all unconsciously join - in the queue or line!

# DIMPLES

We could call her dimples, but that surely is not her name
Those deep impressions in her cheeks surely make her vain
It is the simple fact this dimpled granddaughter lights up my day!
You know those deep dimples are genetic most scientists say . . .
I think God made them on purpose, to make us smile too!
Because with each laugh, smile or smirk we love her a little more
Even babysitting for hours is not really a chore,
You see, it is like a sweet reminder to smile every day
A cosmetic lasting love stamp without a surgeon's fee
A reminder to doting Nonnas, Grandmas, Yia Yais & Nanas just like me!

# AN ANTIDOTE FOR DEPRESSION

There is no magic formula or pill to stop the pain
A fix is impossible, you will search in vain
But I do have a good suggestion as my antidote for depression
Call your friends who are lonely . . . Tell your grandkids a corny joke
Eat eggs for breakfast but leave out the yolk
Smile when you are sad, cover up the tears
Do an act of kindness; it'll alleviate some fears . . .
Say you're sorry, even if you're not wrong!
Say abundant prayers to keep your faith real strong
Ignore the crass curses, deaf to all bad news . . .
The exaggerations and complaints will only give the blues!
Make a point to say "Thank you" - even when they seldom do the same
Your hugs and compliments will never be thought lame
Join the conversation - about cinema and classic books . . .
Don't reveal the endings to avoid the dirty looks
Although you are an expert, admit you could be wrong
Although you hate their music, learn the words to that song!
It is easy to love your kids & grandchildren, so spend some quality time
Write love notes & poems like this one; they don't have to rhyme!
The antidote to depression is to see things always right
Smile and think positive, and tomorrow will be bright!

# THE DATING DILEMMA

1, 2, 3, 4 - What kind of date are you looking for?
(Start with one that doesn't snore!)
5, 6, 7, 8 - Employed, rich & witty would make a good date!
5, 10, 15, 20 – My friends say "A date should have money"
(My mother says "A date should be funny!")
10, 20, 30, 40 – Confident, smart, but not too haughty,
A, B, C, D & E - Every person needs a partner, you see!
F, G, H, I, & J – Same race, same age, same politics - some say
K, L, M, & N – A godly person, I'll defend!
O, P, Q, R, S - This dating dilemma gives me stress!
T, U, V, W, & X - A good date should be more than sex
What is left? Y & Z!
Like doing the New York Times crossword puzzle
IMPOSSIBLE!!!
Don't you AGREE?

# HAPPINESS IS . . .

Happiness is an ephemeral joy
We wish we could capture as a girl or boy
For girls - it might be having great hair
For boys - being good at sports without a care

It is so many things for the adults and teens
Like movies, monopoly, and munching on chips
Getting compliments, trophies, awards or great tips

Happiness is part of the American dream
New cars, new clothes, new romances for some
For kids? Well, simply ice cream!

I think happiness is often so simple
A kiss, tickle, or joke, can cause a sweet dimple
Floating on water, blowing bubbles in the air
Staying up late & waking late without a care!

Swimming with dolphins, petting lambs at the zoo
Skinny dipping, eating cake batter, petting a cat
Pillow fights with scattered feathers . . .
Kissing on the couch – imagine that!

Chocolates and salted nuts always top my list
But a cold beer and hot dogs can't be missed
Licking the icing before guests arrive

Having a Piña Colada or cocktail way before five
Watching a movie classic is a treat
Snatching the last lobster roll or sparerib can't be beat!

Such minor things can make us smile,
Like threading a needle that takes a while.
What makes you happy, is it money or love?
Or is it the blessings of health that come from above?

Treasure and cherish each magic moment, you see
For Happiness is a tiny taste of Heaven for you and me!

# BEYOND THE DIRTY WINDOWS

How much beauty lies beyond the dirty windows, I now see
We spend our lives making seperficial choices, hopefully you agree!
We work from dawn to dusk and save for a rainy day
We give gifts profusely and hope thanks is on its way
We speak words of kindness but often there is a blade
Our jeaousy and selfishness, we hide in the dimmest shade . . .
If only our wisdom came early, - not after fifty years
How much pain would be erased by our abundant tears
We all start our lives with beauty, a baby is just a bloom
Imperfection and misfortune clearly comes too soon
Nature is all powerful and has its own great plan
It is us who invade its deepest caves and the culprit is surely man!
We think we are making our lives better, stealing from the earth its gold
Then surprised when resources are depleted – nothing left to be sold . . .

That crystal clear water I waded in as a child –

                            is now polluted by nasty things

The precious clean air overcome with smog –

                            fossil fuel burning often brings

What happened to the sweet song bird? He doesn't answer my call.

What happened to our cherished Spring & our abbreviated breezy Fall?

Must it take a lifetime to realize the basic lesson for us all

Treat the earth like your precious child

Watch and wonder at its grace . . .

Look beyond the dirty windows at the beauty there is

Acknowledging what mankind only can plunder,

I realize now is a shared disgrace!

# SEVEN IS HEAVEN

"Seven is heaven" . . . I tell my friends, but none of them agree!
Would you have seven chidren in this crazy world like me?
I believe it wasn't all planned of course, but an act of God
Five girls and two boys by 33 would make me seem quite odd
Although my babies were all the most beautiful in town . . .
Some critics looked and wondered "Is she crazy?" with a frown
Sleepless nights, ten thousand diapers, falls and fevers, you may have guessed
Yet, I was very young, in love, and believed I was so very blessed
My friends came for dinner, loved the excitement, then rushed home
Probably called their mother or psychiatrist on the phone
What is wrong with her? Doesn't she yearn to have a break?
With cleaning, laundry, cooking and homework, she's exhausted
          For Goodness sake!

But I would often brag how well my brilliant sons played ball
And praised my five gorgeous daughters who had no faults at all . . .
It could be I'm an optimist or armored against all pain . . .
It could be that the hugs and laughter of so many children made me vain
"Lucky" is one word to describe the seven wonders of my life
Each, with special talents that help me forget life's strife
Now, that I am older, I guess I am a little more distressed
With nearly twelve grandchildren, world conflicts, & little money to invest
I turn to all my photos and memories and say to my dear friends . . .
"Seven is heaven," my favorite motto, I'll defend!

Printed in the United States
By Bookmasters